Powerboat Racing

by Jim Gigliotti

Published by The Child's World®
1980 Lookout Drive
Mankato, MN 56003-1705
800-599-READ
www.childsworld.com

The Child's World®: Mary Berendes, Publishing Director
Shoreline Publishing Group, LLC: James Buckley Jr.,
    Production Director
The Design Lab: Design and production

ISBN 9781609731816
LCCN 2011940084

Photo credits: Cover: AP/Wide World
Interior: AP/Wide World: 7, 20, 28; Corbis: 12, 19;
dreamstime.com: Tatiana Edrenkina 4, Nikolaev 8, 15,
16, Kaikai 23; Andrew Gryuc, 27; iStock, 11;
HORBA, 24.

Printed in the United States of America

Table of Contents

Sami Seliö roars ahead in his Formula 1 powerboat.

CHAPTER ONE

Spectacular Speed!

The engine noise is incredible as Sami Seliö skims along the top of the water. He's driving his sleek Mad-Croc powerboat. His 400-**horsepower** motor makes a high-pitched whir as the boat zips along at almost 140 miles per hour (225 kilometers per hour). Seliö is racing in the F1 H2O World Championships' Grand Prix in 2010 at Abu Dhabi.

Fans line the edges of the waterway. All the other boats have been cleared away for safety. The course for the racers is shown by bright orange **buoys**. Seliö guns his engine to reach top speed. Then he has to slow down to make a tight turn.

Can he make it?

With inches to spare, he makes it. Seliö cuts a hard left turn around a buoy. His boat sends up a huge stream of water as he heads for the checkered flag . . . and victory. His top **rival**, Jay Price, of the U.S., is in hot pursuit. In the end, Price can't catch the "Finnish Flyer." Seliö wins for the second time on the eight-event 2010 schedule. A week later, Seliö gets enough points for finishing second at another event. That gives him the season title . . . by only six points! It's the closest season championship in 10 years.

Seliö (center) celebrates another win, joined by Jay Price and Ahmed Al Hameli.

Powerboats race side by side around curving courses.

Welcome to the world of powerboat racing, where drivers compete in a high-speed sport in powerful machines. Powerboat racers hurtle their machines at death-defying speeds. Yet as we'll see, only a tiny portion of their lightweight, double-**hulled catamarans** touch the water. They race side-by-side with other powerboats, sometimes within inches of each other. They do all this while driving through **plumes** of water that make it very hard to see. One wrong move, and the result can be a dangerous crash.

Some people compare these high-tech powerboats and their drivers to Formula 1 (F1) race cars. Those are the European-based open-wheel racers driven on twisting road courses. Powerboat teams, however, compare their aces with the pilots of fighter jets. Both jet pilots and powerboat drivers have to do their jobs in **intense** places. They each have to make rapid-fire decisions under pressure. They must also be in top shape to deal with G-forces (see box).

This overhead view shows the two pointed hulls of the F1 powerboat shape.

Older speedboats like these were made of wood, but they still moved fast!

CHAPTER TWO

Modern Machines

Today's racing powerboats have come a long way from the first race boats. Those early boats were made of wood. Those boats could really motor, but the plywood easily broke apart. Drivers were often injured or killed in accidents of the **flimsy** craft.

In today's boats, plywood has been replaced by a blend of **synthetics**. These are very lightweight but super strong. Some of those products are carbon fiber and Kevlar. How strong is Kevlar, for instance? It's the same material used to make vests that protect soldiers from bullets.

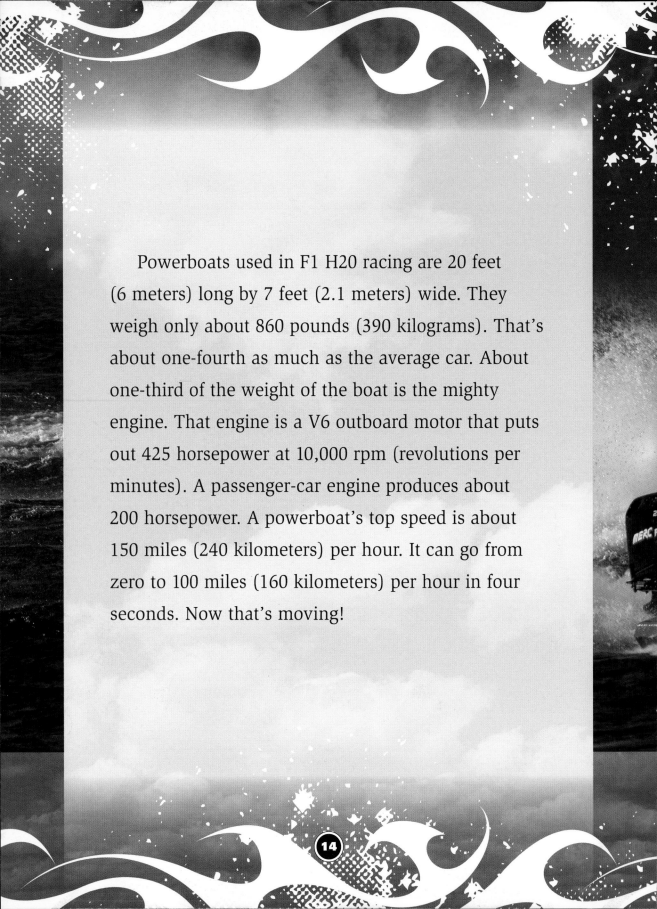

Powerboats used in F1 H20 racing are 20 feet (6 meters) long by 7 feet (2.1 meters) wide. They weigh only about 860 pounds (390 kilograms). That's about one-fourth as much as the average car. About one-third of the weight of the boat is the mighty engine. That engine is a V6 outboard motor that puts out 425 horsepower at 10,000 rpm (revolutions per minutes). A passenger-car engine produces about 200 horsepower. A powerboat's top speed is about 150 miles (240 kilometers) per hour. It can go from zero to 100 miles (160 kilometers) per hour in four seconds. Now that's moving!

Powerful engines let these boats churn at high speeds through and over the water.

The boat moves faster by riding a thin cushion of air beneath its hull.

When a powerboat racer **accelerates**, the front of the boat lifts off the water. Only a few inches of the boat remain on the surface! How does it go so fast? A cushion of air fills the space between the hull and the water. The boat speeds along on that cushion. The powerboat pilot has no brakes. His only tools are a way to go fast and a way to steer. However, he also has a team working with him. That team includes a crew chief, mechanics, and others. They alert him to dangers on the course. If something is in the water, a yellow light in the boat tells the driver to slow down. A red light tells him to return to the dock. Guess what the green light means . . .

Powerboat racing can be dangerous. However, teams work very hard to make sure their pilots are as safe as possible. New technology makes the sport safer than ever. All F1 racers have to wear the Head and Neck Support System, or HANS for short. A collar sits on the racer's shoulders. It attaches to his helmet and to his seat. It prevents the racer's head from whipping around in a crash.

Here's a good look at the cockpit of the powerboat.
The strong windows and frame protect the pilot.

Pilots must be able to quickly escape in case of an accident, or, here, in case of a fire.

The pilots drive while inside a cockpit. It's covered by a windscreen that is super-strong. It also has an air bag. This helps the cockpit float in case of a crash. There is also air for the driver to breathe. Just in case, the Osprey rescue team is at the ready. That's a team of professional scuba divers who specialize in powerboat-race rescues.

Plus, drivers have to pass a special test to be able to compete. In this test, their cockpit is put underwater. The drivers have to get out of their seat belts. Then release the canopy and swim to the surface. Then they have to do it blindfolded! This practice helps drivers stay calm in an emergency.

With amazing boats, years of training, and all this gear to keep them safe, that just leaves one thing for drivers to do: Go fast!

CHAPTER THREE

World's Best

Sami Seliö's F1 championship in 2010 was the second world title of his career. His first came in 2007.

He and the other top drivers take part in a racing series that takes them around the world. Races are held in Europe, the Middle East, and the Far East. Most seasons have 10 or 12 races. F1 races each last about 30 minutes over a 2,000-meter course. Much like in auto racing, pilots compete for pole position (the best starting position) on the first day of the two-day event. Then they line up for the big race on the second day.

In 2010, 12 teams from 11 nations took part in the series. The pilots each get points for where they finish in each race. The higher the finish . . . the more points they earn. At the end of the long, tough season, the pilot with the most points wins the title.

This race was in Purajaya, Indonesia, one of many beautiful places that hold F1 races.

Betty Cook was the first woman to win a world championship in powerboat racing.

The 2011 F1 schedule includes stops in Qatar, Portugal, Russia, Ukraine, China, and the United Arab Emirates.

Italian driver Guido Cappellini dominated the F1 championship series for almost two decades. In 2009, the Italian won the world title for the tenth time in 17 years. Then he retired from the sport. It was no easy ride to the top for Cappellini. He wrecked his boat often early in his career. He was even nicknamed "Crashallini."

In the days before the F1 series started, American Don Aronow and Italian Vincenzo Balestrieri were among the winners of several world championships. That list also includes Betty Cook. She was the most successful female powerboat racer ever. She was a three-time American champion. She also won world titles in 1977 and 1979.

There's more to competitive powerboat racing than just the F1 level. In the United States, powerboat racing is run by the American Power Boat Association. The APBA sanctions events in various classes, including the Offshore Super Series (OSS). ChampBoat racing also holds events throughout the United States. They race smaller versions of the powerful F1 boats. The most successful American ChampBoat racer in recent years is Shaun Torrente. He was the ChampBoat Rookie of the Year in 2006. The Florida native was just 14 when he began racing MiniGT powerboats in 1992. In 2011, he made his **debut** in the F1H20 series.

Shaun Torrente is one of today's best American drivers.

The crowd fills the shore as an F1 race growls to a start!

It costs a lot of money to race powerboats. Those powerful engines are expensive! Some teams in F1 H2O get money from their country's government. Others, like Sam Seliö's championship boat, need **sponsors** to help. Luckily, though, fans don't have to worry about raising money to enjoy powerboat racing. This is one extreme sport that is as much fun to watch as it is to play! The boats' awesome power is an amazing sight to see...and sound to hear! Plus, you can't beat a day in the sunshine near the water!

Glossary

accelerates—increased speed, goes faster

buoy—a floating marker in the water

catamarans—boats with two hulls

debut—first appearance

flimsy—easily broken

horsepower—the unit by which motors are measured

hull—the frame, or body, of a boat

intense—very stressful

plumes—resembling a feather

rival—a person or team one often battles in sports

sponsors—companies that pay money to help sports teams

synthetics—man-made materials

BOOKS

Powerboats (Pull Ahead Books)
By Lisa Bullard (2004, Lerner Publications)
This book gives very young readers their first introduction to the world
of powerboats.

Super Fast Boats (Ultimate Speed)
By Mark Dubowski (2006, Bearport Publishing)
Racing powerboats aren't the only speedy vehicles on water.
Learn about more record-setting vehicles in this book.

WEB SITES

For links to learn more about extreme sports: **childsworld.com/links**

Note to Parents, Teachers, and Librarians: We routinely verify our Web
links to make sure they are safe and active sites. So encourage your
readers to check them out!

Index

About the Author

Jim Gigliotti is a former editor at the National Football League. He has written more than 50 books about sports for youngsters and adults.